Melissa

Blinks

Melissa Blinks

A Journey of Unity, Becoming & Transformation

CULLEN SIRGOOL & SHELLY-ANN MELECIA HAMILTON-SIRGOOL

From a speck unseen, she came to be,

A whisper once, now vast as one can see,

Was she a speck or a star?

Truth is revealed from near and far.

She rose through silence into sound,

A pulse that shaped all space around,

Not here to seek, nor to impress

But stand in truth, and simply express.

She moved with grace, as a dancer's flame,

Aligned with source, yet still the same,

And in her blink, all came to see

The whole in one, in unity.

She left as softly as she came,

Yet nothing, ever, stayed the same.

Table of Contents

merci

Melissa Blinks

Melissa appeared on everyone's radar as little more than a faint impression, that of a speck, a spot on a screen, if you will, and small enough to be overlooked. As with most unrecognizable, negligible previous specks before her, not much attention was given. She shared the sun and the night as any regular day would. Yet no one could have guessed that such a small, quiet presence would soon alter everything that followed. What appears insignificant at first glance sometimes carries within it blueprints for transformation, as with most.

As a speck, Melissa felt that longing to explore her fullest potential with her abundant offerings. There was an ache, a quiet undertone of unfulfillment that was now peeking at a glimpse of maturity, blossoming into purpose.

What once felt like an unrecognizable opportunity was maturely repackaged, thus representing limitless strength in sounds with unknown acting potentials. Sounds in acts purposefully remembering all can equally contribute to the whole as one.

From the speck she was, Melissa grew into the fullest of sizes with an expansive centrifuging force field of wind and rain blanketing the separated communities. This blanket will later be recognized as the ultimate symbol of purpose by adding meaning to unity in the community. Stories, whether his or hers, favored Melissa's rapid growth of strength and vigor like none other. At this magnitude, five out of five, she was now undeniable to one and all.

Melissa was now a part of everyone's construct, woven into the very thought like a familiar piece of fabric expected to be found in every home. Home is the foundation of families on which communities are elevated. For Melissa, a home, regardless of its size, significance, or status, was never seen as merely a shelter for its occupants. For her, homes are where the heart is, and Melissa entered them with pure reverence that was energetically solely hers. One that commanded everyone's attention, gazing fixatedly on her arrival forecasted from her current path. A fixation stemming from many contributing factors that played such major roles in her current presence and trajectory.

Gone were the days of being an insignificant piece of lint to all; no longer was she fragilely unseen or unrecognizable. With all this attention drawn to her, it was time for everyone to prepare for her arrival. With the current positioning, there was a shift of all gazes towards her. The stage was set for her arrival with a couple of pondering questions that no one could have anticipated or foretold.

How will she express herself?

What resonance would she bring?

The air thickened with expectation. In the pause between her arrival and her performance, everyone held their breath not in fear, but in recognition... as the air shifted. The ground sensed it first, then the walls, then everything else that stood witness. Melissa's presence hummed with powerful energy, the kind that precedes revelations. She had gathered herself completely, drawn all her fragmented pieces into a single point of focus.

What happens when a force of nature fully matures and simply decides to be?

To encounter such an expression is to step into a realm where mastery and mystery coexist, inseparably. The answer begins not with thunder, but with a tremor. Small at first, the sounds described as wind mastery began to release into the waiting silence. This is how Melissa began, and we have seen what small becomes when given room to grow. The vine that nurtured her fruit now bends towards new soil. Melissa always knew of her gifts and capabilities, as she Blinks!

At this introductory moment in time, when her eyes open, they are not seeking. They are focused.

Anticipated Arrival

Anticipated Arrival

Melissa's arrival was never scheduled, summoned, or arranged by anyone; she arrived uninvited, unbidden, and as such, she required no permission or escorted validation. Her entry was not learned; it was remembered through timelines of timeless ancestral synchronized memories.

With such limitless depth of access to memories rooted in ancient connections of origin, when Melissa's expressions were performed, they became ageless in real time. A performance holding the imprint of every memory in all art forms touched. A boundless vastness similar to an endless horizon of incomprehensible transformations. Given her space and her time horizon, she arrived as who she was destined to be for the current anticipated act.

Anticipation without memes of anxiety or disappointment, as that was an impossibility! Her performance will not be for review, but the deepest, truest expression of her soul as truths. As one of her truths, even as a speck-star, she knew she was a vital piece to the puzzling contribution as a whole.

Everyone knew something big was coming, but what exactly? The sense of anticipation was jovial and light, almost playful, as if the world was holding its breath, waiting for her to bust a move. The air almost felt a little different, like a soft whisper being carried on the breeze as Melissa arrived in a style of majesty. Her arrival flowed and was never rushed; it followed an unpredictable pattern. No matter how much they tried to anticipate her schedule, Melissa arrived on her own divine time. Wonderment followed such an aura.

There was a quiet sense of curiosity building, as if the land where her stage anchored was also waiting for her appearance. Melissa's unprecedented arrival was permanently bound to bring a fresh wave of change, and that certainty was enough to keep everyone intrigued. Some pondered. Would it be as expected, or would something new unfold? Either way, one thing was certain: Melissa's arrival.

Her arrival was an event rooted deep within the land, below the lowest depth of the sea and all air, part of a culmination that had been unfolding for millennia. That culminating force, showcasing her strength upon arrival, not only shaped the land but also the communal people. They had learned to track and predict her predecessors, yet she arrived in grand style in what seemed like her own time zone.

Preparation for her arrival had been limited to speculative narratives, which many dismissed entirely, given the misinformation and its ineffectiveness, borrowing from past performances, from the likes of Melissa. Upon arrival, they did not know her, not even by the slightest inkling. That unfamiliarity was due to the disconnection from the piece of the whole that carried Melissa.

Even though unfamiliar, Melissa embodied stories of greatness within her, with echoes of magnificence demonstrated from predecessors such as her relative, Gilbert. Similarly, future little speck-stars are poised to surpass Melissa's talent with gifts way beyond anyone's wildest imagination, in anticipation of any meaningful preparation of any kind. With such awareness, she approached her performance with patience in her stride, grace in her stillness, and magnificence that erupted the atmosphere like an awakening.

In the final moments of her approach, as she sets her eyes on her stage, there was the calming before the storm effect, as if being in the eye of it. A pause in shear force winds granted an additional time window for any last-minute preparation. Not long after, the air suddenly charged, and finally, the performance was about to begin. Melissa stepped forward unmistakably, ready to perform, not to impress, but to fully express herself. An expression of her truest self, unburdened by expectations, pure in its authenticity in all facets of delivery.

Performance

The Performance

The moment had come. It was showtime. Now was the time for Melissa to become one with her stage and everything on and around it. All preparations culminated in this divine moment, fulfilling her destiny as a revelation of all her truths, however interpreted. Her awareness widened, considering the responsibility of this privileged opportunity as she took the stage. She pondered the future speck-stars who may one day follow her theatrics. A sight and a feeling of presence to behold for those in attendance, as her performance began and bloomed into angelic formations.

As in the beginning and throughout, Melissa sang her best songs on the perfect pitch. Each note was crafted with precision and intention, honing it so tight that every depth of nuance in each act was profoundly felt by all. The lightning-technec incorporation within her sounds added deeper soulful layers, where the majority who experienced the time with Melissa described it as soul-resounding.

The trees responded first. They swayed, twisted, and danced in Melissa's whirlwind voice, like a robin navigating a storm, tuning to a rhythm only she could fathom, much less command. Some trees gifted branches, leaves, fruits, and roots without hesitation or apprehension of maturity as a token of her performance. Many others contributed, some prematurely or reluctantly, much later to her performance with valuables of their own.

Participation became involuntary and more of a natural response as the performance unfolded like none other. Even Melissa was surprised herself by how seamlessly it all came together for her, given her preparation and everyone's contribution, which now provided the very materials for the revealing masterpiece production.

In some special moments, Melissa became not just a performer but a conduit; a living revelation of what is possible through self-expression in character in ageless real time. She danced in the wind rhythmically to these lightning-technec sounds, at times spinning completely, matching the performance as only she could define being in her creative divinity. Every note, spin, light, and vibration of sound became a part of something larger than herself. It was as though the very universe had paused to witness the purest expression of itself in unison with all its timeless, boundless possibilities.

In that unique moment, Melissa was mastering the presence of life mysteries in an expressive artistic living performance. It was as though Melissa morphed, where she became one with the light force, the wind, the deepest of our seas, and all the earth beneath her. Melissa displayed the grandest expression of life with the force of nature that authored every act that ever existed. Such an ideal embodiment of everything that had come before and everything that was yet to come.

Her purest form of choreographed movements resonated far beyond her stage. Deep within the core and far beyond the furthest parts of the foundation of earth, air, heavens, waters, every known and unknown being, and all else, inclusive of the watchers as active participants. Compared to her predecessors, her performance felt otherworldly, with flawless authority unlike any other previously experienced. This was one of the best and strongest performances ever witnessed. Which could only have been made possible with the guidance of her all, God, everything, one true source.

One constant truth was evident throughout Melissa's performance; her only influence and guide was her source, nothing else! The unimaginable unfolded before all, as Melissa showcased her gifts in her fullest glory.

Everyone was compelled to partake, drawn by the sheer magnitude of the moment, who she represented, her power, brilliance, and magnificence.

Her blinking translated into days and nights. Each movement, and every minuscule moment of her performance, was pleasing and aligned seamlessly as it could ever possibly be. Understanding the act, or not, it is now undeniably connected as one iconic piece of the source through stories, whether his or hers.

A recorded prophetic performance showcasing life's stories in their purest of truths. An expression of self-revelation in fulfilling moments of self- awareness, in real time.

Curtains

Curtains Down

As Melissa set her sights on her next stage, a quiet knowing settled within her; she had given her best. The outcome was unprecedented, unmatched; a recorded proof that nothing like this had ever been seen, witnessed, or experienced. Some acts within the performance carried such power that they required an encore, summoned not by request but a shared pull by energy alone, a resonance of itself.

With the curtains down, the aftermath of Melissa's performance rivaled any limitless budget production not crafted by hand but by essence. When the final rendition of her performance settled, what remained was a transformed atmosphere in this hemisphere for such a moment as this. The magnified impact of Melissa was credited to her energized connection to the source as the catalyst.

Everything felt elevated as if each detail was heightened and meticulously arranged with a precision that only her ALL could orchestrate. What had once drifted loosely across communities was now brought together.

The majority were replaced completely or transformed anew, while others shifted in various directions by either retreating or advancing. With every movement coordinated, every element was perfectly aligned, mimicking a true symphony of precision.

Melissa's performance attracted many accolades, including the grandest stage ever known by anything or anyone historically in these communal parts of the world. Yet with every grand display comes the inevitable curtains down and changing of views. Communities were now looking at a new territory, given the task ahead of rebuilding using unknown puzzle pieces, as a normalizing reference. Restoration after such a grand performance as Melissa's will be no simple undertaking. It is one that will require faith, the heart, mind, and heavy lifting wherever possible, given this new era of restructuring and restoration opportunities in the aftershock following Melissa.

Opportunities to reflect on the best commonality practices of Melissa's ALL amongst a deeper-rooted connection for a stronger future. The necessity of maintaining that depth of connection to ALL is the highest expression of love in togetherness with source, that of Melissa, other speck-stars, and each other. Melissa's performance offered a blueprint of oneness; a glimpse of what becomes possible when that powerful reconnection is restored.

Some may argue this is how it was always meant to be. It's the natural state of things being free from barriers and challenges that sustain this disconnection as one community. Others may not agree but instead choose to welcome the reconfirmation of status quo affirmations, given the very facts. All encompassing, our space is lovingly energized by the source for sharing amongst all communities.

Melissa's expression and impact extended far beyond what anyone anticipated when the curtains came down in the final act. The source that fueled her became the very force guiding this communal, resilient restoration using these newfound era pieces. Families are the common denominator for the shared love within effective, efficient, sustainable, and impactful representation of the commonality in communities. This new era of foundation is dynamically in place for all to thrive, now through eternity as one harmonious community.

Faithful restoration after such a monumental event will be another masterpiece like Melissa's symphony, where each player purposefully satisfies their role in these newfound harmonies.

UNiTy
PiECES

Unity Pieces

Melissa, as with her source, could not relate to the unknown divisions of the game and their players as a community. All being a puzzling obscurity due to the disconnection experienced over time with these immensely separated communities, each other, and that of speck-stars. Ideally, she represents something more intricate; a gradual shift in perception, unfolding over time, rather than simply uniting familiar puzzle pieces into togetherness.

The magnificence of the disconnected pieces together, as showcased through Melissa's performance, was the vision to behold. Each piece intertwines together like a woven knitted quilt; each aspect discovering its true purpose through alignment with the source, rather than other external influences.

Connecting the performing puzzle pieces together clearly flowed fluidly, as everyone positioned themselves in tune with her performance. Thus, creating the masterpiece by connecting these master pieces as provided by the source in many creative shapes, colors, and sounds. This was an evolving composition with intention, timing, and grace. Melissa did not see a puzzle or its masters or its pieces; instead, she saw all connections in real time playing harmoniously, becoming the overall optimal display of performance.

Comfort existed only for some master-players, as Melissa's performance was neither fluctuating nor stagnant; it simply was. It unfolded in her connection with her source and foundation. She moved through the experience with an effortlessness of grace born not of comfort, but of alignment. Her performance followed the only rules that truly mattered; rules not bound by anyone's external guidelines.

The energy signature she displayed remained unchanged as that of the source from the beginning and lingered long after the performance's final note. It was an echo of origins that was untampered and unchangeable. One that remains on the tongue and thoughts of all to this day to be remembered.

A poster performance for the reminder that all puzzle pieces in time will reflect the wholeness to everyone, as it did for Melissa. The resonance of true power in the viewing of all parts of a whole. The pieces, the vagueness, the beauty; without the need of assembling them together by anyone's thought, being natural as the ultimate strategy for sustainability. It is the foundation that best reflects the source of all.

Like the trees, branches, leaves, flowers, petals, blossoms, and in some instances, offering their entirety towards celebrating Mellissa's individuality, while becoming part of one identity in unity as a community. To call on some good references for unity, treat it as you would yourself. If a faint impression of the expression of a speck appears, it might be you. Offer the care and attention you would hope to receive because you never know what the future holds.

This was Melissa's reflection of source in her preparation, growth, and fruition of her performance. No one truly knew her because no one viewed her as a part of the scattered whole, as masterly defined and maintained as one of convenience in fragments. In reflection, so are the puzzle pieces, often unaware, in some cases, of the existence of the other unifying pieces. This disconnection is unsustainable for the fullness of experience in oneness, as family is the ultimate foundation for communities. To thrive, the pieces must awaken each other.

Awareness is the first bridge to unity.

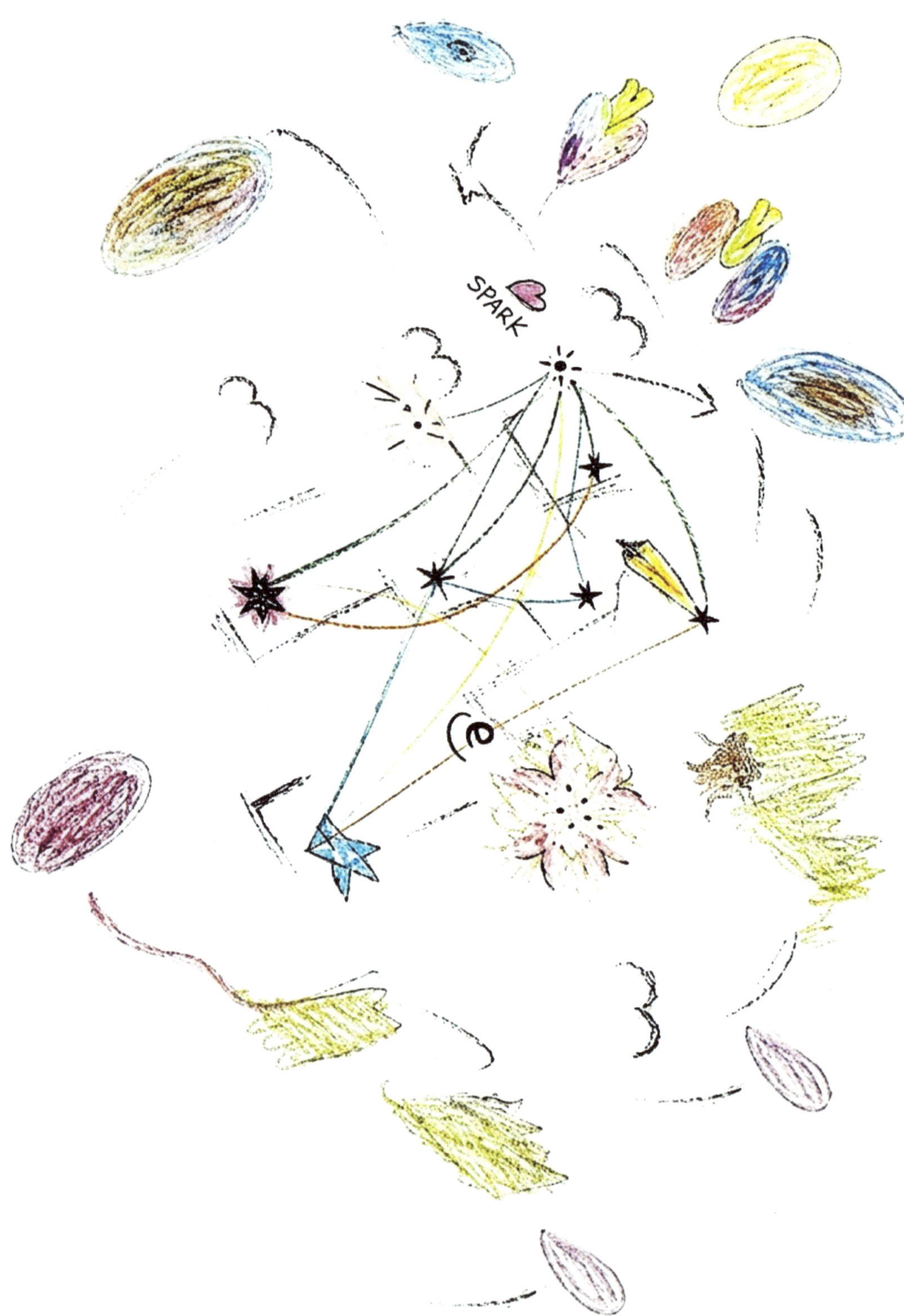

SPARK

Melissa Unites

Melissa's timeless performance revealed how she embodied grace as an expression deeply rooted in her source as an unwavering foundation. Such masterful performances in expression, of that of a puzzle, being a unit in alignment with all pieces. As she traversed her path to another realm, her choreography was a sobering reminder of the possibility when functioning as one (an all-encompassing cell). Her movements did not erase the progress that came before; it illuminated what was always possible in the avail of abilities in unifications.

Her strength remained consistent and steadfast throughout all stages of the experience, even extending beyond Melissa's path. From the smallest acknowledgment to the grandest realization, unlimited possibilities arose from the willingness to unite to dance and sing. These possibilities of unity drastically limit all unwilling to embrace it, regardless of the claim of supreme representation in any style or form. Unity does not require sameness; it requires willingness to participate, contribute, and accept the unique expression of the source within all parts.

The majority are already shaping and sharing the future of unity beyond Melissa. Yet the importance of positions and pieces, always temporary, is best understood through the heavenly vantage point revealed by Melissa. Perspectives endure. Roles shift. Stages dissolve. To see beyond the stage of a single performance is to recognize and include the other stages and horizons in which she partakes, as showcased by Melissa and her trajectory. Her journey teaches that no single stage is final, and no performance exists in isolation. What unfolds on one plain echoes across many, as witnessed and experienced by everyone, as it would in the heavens for all.

The keys to unlocking such a performance as Melissa's are not by requests, but by invitations: ethical preparation, tenacity, gratitude, and a deep appreciation for the whole. These keys are freely offered to those willing to receive and accept them through application. Each piece is uniquely designed to fit seamlessly together, contributing to one collective harmony. Through these contributions, a greater sense of belonging for all is achieved, one that transcends individual moments or stages.

Melissa's performance transcended time, revealing unseen alterations borrowing from the interwoven threading between quilts. Altering prospective realities as all things interweave, thus contributing to the deep embodiment of unity as one unit under the sun in loving and peaceful cohabitation. In this perceived shift in reality, it was as though Melissa's act awakened something profound in those who bore witness to it.

This experience wasn't just a performance; it was a gentle reminder that even the smallest actions can have far-reaching effects. Though the rewards are often given the most attention, they don't always reveal the full picture. The disconnection sometimes overshadows the quiet connections that ripple through the unnoticed, leaving their deeper impact hidden in the spaces where unity should be.

Will Melissa be seen again, in another glory, on another path, on any trajectory? Perhaps the question is not whether she will appear again, but whether she will be recognized, truly recognized for what she represents, and what will be the reaction? Will the witnesses treat another appearance differently, or will they still be limited to the limitations of their current view?

The End

One Transformation

The aftermath of Melissa's performance sparked a renewed vigor across many communities, even those not in her trajectory, traversing to another gracious performance. Her influence traveled beyond barriers and between spaces, awakening motion where stillness once lived. What was touched did not need to witness her directly to be influenced by the change. A feeling of unity in transformation occurred amongst communities far beyond the proximity of experiencing and witnessing Melissa firsthand.

There was an unmistakable beauty in her undeniable presence, a quiet source-field of strength and tenacity, not overwhelming or underwhelming, a stalwart. In that presence lived a deep willingness to fully partake in the source's future, not as a singular ideal, but as a vision for a truly united, loving world. A redefined future as one world shared with nations in nature, naturally exploring all worlds. What once appeared fragmented now gestures toward coherence. There emerges an opportunity to balance the foundation and the energies that best reflect here, now, and forever. Simply a blink in the view of Melissa, much less than the timelessness, in source.

In this fleeting moment, there is an opportunity to align one's highest intentions with the known currents when connecting with each other in perfect love. Blinking stories, whether his or hers, favored how aligned connections can perfectly linger as legacies. What seems like a blink can generate the potential to create ripples that resonate far beyond the present of our presence. Often overlooked, but the most profound transformations quietly unfold in the simplest instances.

As demonstrated by Melissa, the future that remained evident was to align with the source; a notion to note the simplistic possibilities to share and naturally communicate effectively. She needed nothing that was grossly misvalued and fiercely protected for sharing with a few chosen in disconnected communities.

As with the communities in the ancient story of Babel, Melissa's performance transcended language and all other barriers. Her expression required no translation; meaning arrived in its entirety and was understood by all, even those far beyond her presence or trajectories.

No arrangement, nor its execution, could prepare communities for the likes of Melissa or others bearing similar signatures of energy connection with the source. What moves from the source arrives complete. Every movement she made was boundless, leaving a feeling of angelic mystique and celestial power. To encounter such an expression is to step into a realm where mastery and mystery coexist, inseparably. The presence of the magnificence of all worlds offered context for humility, coupled with the above-mentioned notion. Communities now embark on the undertaking of repurposing foundational pillars towards their futuristic angelic performances.

An apex of outcomes of Melissa's performance was a reminder to all that they are one nation under God, as one, and source, in a single blink. The reminder becomes internalized where unity lives in the highest of that of awareness in self and all else.

In the end, Melissa returns not to grandeur, but to the speck from which she first appeared. The transformation from the blueprint is now complete.

What once seemed unrecognizable was now recognized as a necessity for unity as community, a reminder that every beginning carries the weight of becoming. The curtains flow quietly down; the space settles, yet nothing remains the same. For the speck was never alone; it was always part of the whole as a fulfilling cornerstone of an act. And in that recognition, everyone remembers that even the smallest presence, when aligned with the source, holds the power to reshape everything in a single blink.

Melissa Blinks!

Why our book?

Melissa Blinks was written for more than a story. It can serve as a reminder on transformation, exposure, renewal, and the unseen connections that unite us all.

Inspired by living in the Caribbean and South Florida, both resilient communities, whose experience and lifestyle impact are documented. This writing explores documenting disruption as a catalyst for awakening. Storms, both literal and symbolic, have the power to expose what has long been hidden beneath the surface. They clear away weakened foundations, remove barriers, and reveal anew what is necessary for rebuilding with greater intention, strength, and unity.

This is the only way for the emerging new, revisiting the old as the foundation to capture added heights in emerging layers.

Within every season of upheaval exists an opportunity for fresh perspectives, deeper understanding, and renewed purpose. Exposure creates space for reflection. Reflection creates awareness. Awareness creates the possibility for meaningful change. Change is the growth, that of a child and all life.

At the core, Melissa Blinks is an invitation to consider how life's most unexpected, sometimes most difficult, moments can become pathways for connections towards further and greater transformations. We aspire for our book to serve as a reminder that true peace and unity is a viable possibility. Those words were not aligned originally with separation, but from recognizing the value and necessity of every piece within the sustainable whole.

May Melissa's journey be an encouragement to embrace growth, remain open to new understanding, and recognize the quiet power that exists within even the smallest creative speck.